Mr. Biffy's Battle

Richard Tulloch
Illustrated by Christine Ross

CELEBRATION PRESS
Pearson Learning Group

Every lunchtime, on the southwest corner of Market Mall . . .

Mr. Biffy did tricks for the crowd.

Mr. Biffy twisted a bendy balloon into the shape of a sausage dog.

He juggled scarves and balanced an umbrella on his knee.

He played "Oh, Susannah" on the harmonica.

Then Mr. Biffy bowed while people clapped and coins clinked into the battered felt hat in front of him.

Even Sergeant Peebles the policeman sometimes stopped to watch, though he never gave Mr. Biffy any money.

Then as the crowd drifted away to go about their afternoon business, Mr. Biffy shuffled off to the Blue Flamingo Cafe for lunch of Flaky Fish Fillets, with chocolate milk and cake for dessert.

One day, just before lunchtime, Mr. Biffy approached the southwest corner of Market Mall to find a crowd gathered there already.

"Wonderful!" thought Mr. Biffy. "I'm so popular that my audience is waiting for me."

When he drew closer, he saw that the crowd wasn't waiting for him at all. They were watching a lady clown called Fiona the Great, balancing a spinning plate on a silver stick and riding a silver unicycle.

She had just pulled a bunch of silver flowers out of the ear of a man from the audience when Mr. Biffy stepped forward and tapped her on the shoulder.

"Excuse me, young lady," said Mr. Biffy sternly, "but you're right in the middle of my spot. I perform on the southwest corner of Market Mall every lunchtime."

"That may be," replied Fiona coolly, "but this lunchtime, I was here first."

Mr. Biffy was furious.

Just then Sergeant Peebles stepped between the two clowns and put his huge arms around their shoulders.

"A fair thing's a fair thing," he said. "Fiona the Great can do her act until half past twelve. After that it's Mr. Biffy's turn."

So Mr. Biffy had to watch while Fiona the Great played "You Are My Sunshine" on a silver ukulele, drank a glass of water and squirted it out of her buttonhole, and collected a silver top hat full of shiny coins.

Mr. Biffy was **furious!**

He was so angry when it was time for his act, that he squeezed his balloon sausage dog so hard he popped it.

He dribbled into his harmonica so that it would hardly play a note.

He barely collected enough coins to buy a sausage at the Blue Flamingo Cafe.

Worst of all, Fiona the Great was sitting in a corner, eating Flaky Fish Fillets.

"Just you wait till tomorrow, Fiona the Great," muttered Mr. Biffy. "Then I'll show you some real clowning!"

Next morning Mr. Biffy was at the southwest corner of Market Mall extra early.

He began his act by twisting two balloons into the shape of a giraffe.

Then he juggled three carrots while balancing a cabbage on his nose. Then he realized nobody was watching him.

Everyone had crossed over to the northwest corner of Market Mall where Fiona the Great was blowing balls of fire from her mouth.

Even Sergeant Peebles was watching her with a smile from ear to ear.

"There ought to be a law against stealing someone's crowd!" Mr. Biffy told him.

"A fair thing's a fair thing, Mr. B," said Sergeant Peebles. "Besides, that Fiona's not bad, is she?"

Then he dropped a coin into the silver top hat.

Mr. Biffy was **furious!**

He stormed off to the Blue Flamingo Cafe for a cup of tea, which was all he could afford.

And worst of all, Fiona the Great came in and ordered a chocolate milk and cake.

"Just you wait until tomorrow, Fiona the Great," muttered Mr. Biffy. "Then I'll show you some real clowning."

The next morning, Mr. Biffy arrived at Market Mall to find Fiona the Great cracking a silver stockwhip on the northwest corner.

Mr. Biffy went straight to his spot on the southwest corner and smiled to himself as he switched on a huge portable CD player.

The Blue Danube Waltz blasted out across Market Mall while Mr. Biffy twisted a whole box of balloons into a model of the Sydney Harbour Bridge.

A few heads in Fiona's crowd turned to watch.

The CD player blasted out Beethoven's *Fifth Symphony* while Mr. Biffy climbed a tower of chairs and balanced a bucket of water on his forehead.

People started leaving Fiona's crowd and came across to watch Mr. Biffy.

Fiona the Great launched into a magic cooking routine, pulling custard pies from an empty cake tin, but she was no match for Mr. Biffy.

The CD player blasted out the *1812 Overture* while Mr. Biffy juggled five flaming firesticks and caught them behind his back.

The crowd had never seen Mr. Biffy performing so brilliantly.

He was just getting ready to balance a blow-up baseball bat, a blow-up plastic hammer, and a blow-up saxophone, when Fiona the Great tapped him on the shoulder.

She was **fuuurious!!!**

"Steal my crowd, would you?" she screamed at Mr. Biffy. "You know nothing about clowning. You scruffy rag tag!"

"You think you're so smart in your shiny-silver suit," said Mr. Biffy. "You prancing preening peacock!"

Fiona the Great tickled Mr. Biffy's bottom with the blow-up baseball bat.

"Take that, Mr. Boring!"

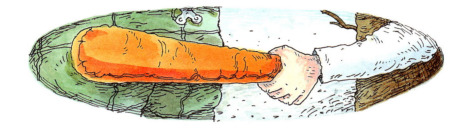

Mr. Biffy tapped Fiona the Great with the blow-up hammer.

"You take that, Fiona, the Not-So-Great!"

"Don't you call me Fiona the Not-So-Great, you big baby!" shrieked Fiona the Great.

She grabbed one of Mr. Biffy's firesticks and hurled it at his head. Mr. Biffy caught it in mid-air and hurled it back at her.

In a moment firesticks were zipping back and forth between them, and the crowd started to clap.

Then a burning firestick slipped from Mr. Biffy's hand and disappeared behind him. He turned to pick it up again but couldn't find it. It was stuck in the back of his baggy pants.

The crowd roared as Mr. Biffy ran round in circles, beating at his trousers with smoke pouring from his bottom.

"Your pants are on fire!" yelled Fiona, and as Mr. Biffy passed her for the third time, she threw the bucket of water over him.

Mr. Biffy was **FUUURIOUSS!!!**

Mr. Biffy turned to chase after Fiona the Great, but just as he did, his wet baggy pants broke their suspenders and fell down around his ankles, so that everyone could see his spotted red underpants.

The crowd howled with laughter.

Fiona the Great doubled over with laughter too until suddenly . . .

Pllltttt!

Her tight silver pants split right up her backside. She was wearing spotted red underpants too!

Mr. Biffy and Fiona the Great were
FUUUUUUURIOUS!!!!

"I'll get you, Miss Fancypants!" growled Mr. Biffy, reaching for a pie.

"I dare you to try, Mr. Scruffy Bottom!" growled Fiona the Great, and she reached for a pie too.

The two clowns ran toward each other, slipped in the water left by the puddle from the bucket, and fell flat on their backs.

The two pies flew up in the air and landed SPLAT! on their faces.

The crowd laughed until tears rolled down their cheeks and clapped until their hands were raw.

Coins rained down into the silver top hat, and the battered old felt hat too.

Mr. Biffy struggled to his feet and reached out his hand to Fiona the Great.

Hand in hand they faced the cheering crowd and bowed.

As the crowd drifted away to go about their afternoon business, Sergeant Peebles put his huge arms around the two clowns' shoulders.

"I'm not a rich man," he said, "but a fair thing's a fair thing, and today I saw real clowning. That act beats the lot!"

He dropped a five dollar bill into each of the two hats.

"Fiona the Great," said Mr. Biffy, "Would you allow me to buy you a lunch of Flaky Fish Fillets at the Blue Flamingo Cafe?"

"Certainly, Mr. Biffy," said Fiona the Great, "if YOU will allow ME to buy you a chocolate milk and cake for dessert."

The next day a new sign was hanging in Market Mall.

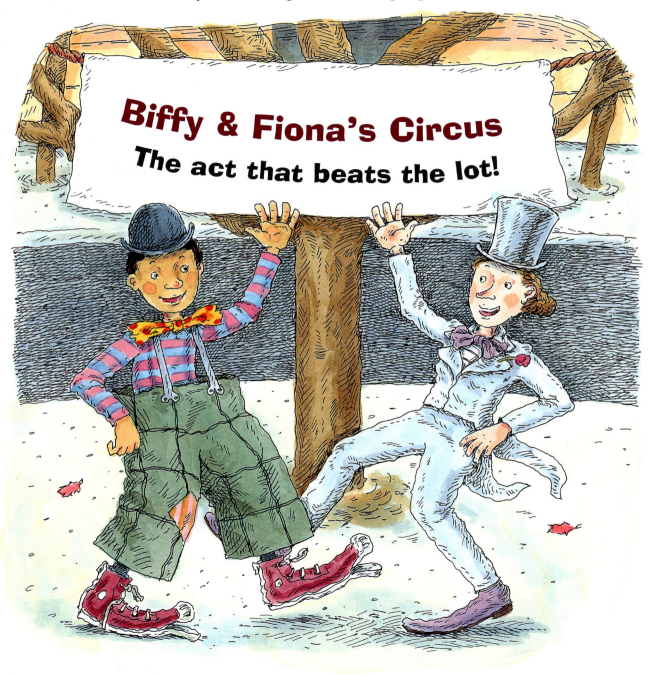